PICKLES AND PARADISE

poems for pickleballers

KRISTIN F. JOHNSON

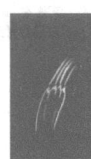

Contents

for my wife
who injured her arm

the community

Partners

the best spouses know
when you really need other
partners for your game

Court Rules

1. Always wear good shoes.
2. When life comes at you, let things bounce before reacting.
3. Some shots are tougher to make than others.
4. You don't have to say sorry every time you make a mistake.
5. Be polite.
6. Wait your turn.
7. Include everyone.
8. Be a teacher, a coach, a partner in play.
9. Don't be so competitive that you get hurt.
10. Say good game when it ends.

Searching

Look in any parking lot--
backing up now no one stops.
Thank yous are seldom heard.
Sorry's an even rarer word.

But, on the pickleball court
you will see nothing of this sort.
No one argues their shot was good.
Whoever received it makes the call.

Players help partners keep the score
No one worries about being on the ball.
When each game ends,
paddle taps between friends.

Playing fair and square, just as it should be.
I know on the court I'll find civility.

Perfect Day

early morning play
afternoon drills with a coach
more play into night

No Point

We introduce ourselves cordially
knowing names will be forgotten
like the score
we can't remember
from point to point.

Court Crush

Barb snatched the last
spot on the paddle rack
next to the blue paddle
she knew belonged to Bill.

In My Experience

Everyone is welcome on the court
whether you are good or bad at the sport.
Whether your serve lands in the kitchen
or you return the ball, and your shot isn't in,
as long as you don't act like a spoilsport,
you will have much pickled support.

Networking

Networking means
something else
on the court
It means keeping toes to the line
staying close to the kitchen
blocking the ball
when it flies over the net.
Networking means
not being afraid of the ball
coming at you fast
working your way
to send a lob or a dink.
Both unreturnable.
Think fast.
Network.

Acrostic

Please protect me
Against
Deadly balls,
Dreaded shots
Landing at my feet
Ending the point too soon.

Attitude Shift

game
fun, friendly
volley, stretch, anticipate
ball, kitchen, paddle, point
lunge, hit, focus
fearsome, treacherous
sport

Modern-Day Tennis Courts

dog park
kid coral
weed garden
with ghastly overgrowth
of thriving things —

but Dandelions,
Canada thistle,
and Creeping Charlie
were the wrong
thriving things —

invading a time capsule
in plain sight

Tom's Request

Tom posted a message to the TeamReach
display: *Darn, I forgot to bring donuts today.*

He hoped someone would read it and take his
hint, and understand what he really meant.

Dunkin, Byerly's, Cub, or someplace new;
beggars couldn't be choosers-- any donut
would do.

Chris brought brownies his wife had baked.
Retired Bruce bought cookies to celebrate.

And though Tom didn't get what he asked
from his team, he still enjoyed his Boston
cream.

She Forgot

Jenny could never
remember the score,
if she had served,
or what her paddle was for.

She worried each week
that her memory was failing,
but all the others'
memories were also bailing.

The memory issues,
they seemed epidemic.
The worst thing they'd seen
since the goddamn pandemic.

Let's forget the score!
Jenny yelled with affection.
Getting to the court,
was the important recollection.

Brad's Bad Day

Brad's bad day
started with the wind.
It took his shots places
that didn't stay in.

Brad hit that orb
with such driving force,
When the wind died down,
the ball dropped off course.

Then that evil wind
blew his ball far away.
So, Brad left with his paddle;
he'd play another day.

The Actuary

Steve played the game
ne'er with chagrin
He knew his fate,
the games he might win.

He'd worked hard thirty years,
figured numbers and odds.
So, as each game ended,
he gave a knowing nod.

Because he studied stats,
and how chance applied,
he knew what to expect,
and took outcomes in stride.

One day Steve was wrong--
he had lost a game.
But his calculations weren't off;
no equations had changed.

Pickleball had thrown
his estimations out of whack.
His profession no longer helped him.
Statistics did *not* have his back.

The moral of the story
is simple logic for some:
it's how often you play--
not how often you've won.

Visionary

In abandoned shopping malls,
the open floors of anchor stores
would make great courts.
Bright fluorescent lights aid
aging eyes to see sidelines clearly.
Checkout counters could serve
as check-ins for court times
and water bottle sales.
Sock and underwear end caps
could become paddle racks.

Sweet Spot

At thirteen,
I rode my light blue Schwinn
down to South Glen
where tennis courts waited
for players.

At thirteen,
all we had to do to make friends
was say, "Hey. Do you want to play?"
and a game would commence.

That year, the sweet spot wasn't
just a place on your tennis racket,
it was also when
you were old enough to go off alone
on your bike
but not old enough to get a job.

The sweet spot these days is
a place on your paddle
and being young enough
to be agile for play
and being old enough
to appreciate the pickled years ahead.

Puckering

I saw an ad for
pickle-flavored jellybeans.
I puckered. *Too far!*

Helping Hand

I was donning gym clothes
on my first game day
when I realized I didn't have
a paddle to play.

I checked Play it Again
and also online
but nary a paddle
was I able to find.

I showed up anyway
though my shopping trip botched.
I sighed a great sigh
Figuring I'd just watch.

'Til my partner said,
Hey! I know what to do!
She produced from her bag
not one paddle, but two.

I learned a good lesson:
just give a yelp.
When you are in need,
Picklers will help.

the weathered

KRISTIN F. JOHNSON

Determined

when leaves fall on court
diehard players rake and blow
undeterred from play

Net New

That year, winter was
unseasonably
late.
The city put the nets away
too soon.
When we saw temps
in the 50s,
players stormed
to the courts.
Some brought nets
from home
unwilling to miss out
on winter's delay.

False Spring

Oh, how I wish the weather would turn
Mother nature teases us with her range
making temps jump up early
only to plummet to freezing
again.

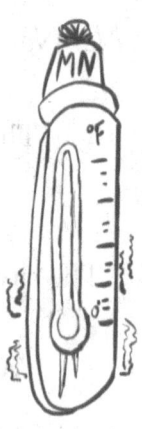

Sunny Sonnet

Some people in winter suffer SAD.
But the gray effect never stole *my* glee.
I recall the many hours outside I had.
Did they keep SAD from finding me?

I took for granted those days outside
Until playing pickleball made me see
The sun and wind and elements belied.
How splendid was time in light reverie.

In fact, the more hours I spent outdoors,
the further from wary I found my mood.
Some players bet against my happy stores,
Still, my winning cheerfulness ensued.

Perhaps being outside and the sunny court
combined
Helped keep lowly moods at bay, preserved
my peace of mind.

The Yankee

I long for the days of the outdoor court
alas for the snow's melt we wait.
Our summer days always seem too short,
Minnesota being a northernmost state.

But soon the robin will tweet its song,
the warmth of spring casting snow away.
I'd move south during winter seasons long,
but a Yank I was born and a Yank I shall stay.

Sometimes the Wind

Hard to say on a windy day
which way the ball will go.
You make your best guess,
but you never really know.

Sometimes it helps,
pushes your serve in the square.
Sometimes it sends your shot
where you haven't a prayer.

But one thing's for sure,
no matter how the wind blows:
Sometimes it's your friend,
sometimes a foe.

Ode to Rain

When the rains come, and they always do,
the court becomes a slipping danger,
but the true pickleballer will not eschew,
even as conditions make for a game changer.

On the courts we will descend,
our cleaning crew like a pack.
We'll squeegee, leaf blow till the end,
And claim our spot on the paddle rack.

Blown Away

leaves fall on the court
our days outside are numbered
for now, blowers work

Off-Court Cinquain

Thunder
rolled in faster
than we had expected
so, we grabbed our paddles
and ran.

Frustration

another leaf fell
on the court under the elm
just after I swept

Losing Lethargy

Once fluffy piles of snowdrift melt away
When winter's white finally ceases flight
To the paved court again I'll make my way
The paddle rack on the hillside and in sight.

My winter insulation follows me
a weight around my trunk until it's shed
a lighter, agile player I'll soon be
my lust for playing now what's being fed.

When friends bring donut treats to share
I will look away, steady in my aim
Or maybe cut in half I will bear
That one glazed morsel, fueling my next
game.

I know the way to lose my lethargy—
Hitting the court ramps up my energy.

Two Squeegees

raindrops won't stop us
two squeegees methodically
push water down court

Long Winter

the courts are covered
by white blankets, 'til spring
players hibernate

Shadow Court Problems

My transition lenses
kept the sun from my eyes,
but as the day wore on
I had a surprise--

The lenses didn't change back
as fast as I needed.
I wanted a time out,
but play proceeded.

The shadiness made
the court double dark,
With the green ground gone,
I missed my mark.

But there is a lesson
to learn from that day:
Be wary which shades
you wear when you play.

the unapologetic

Gutsy

My paddle is dusty.
My skills are rusty.
Guess I'm back to beginner's luck.
But… that also means I'll have pluck.
Time to show up, and be gutsy!

For Sale

The excuses, they lined up so well
for why Ginny's game went to hell.
The wind took the ball
beyond the mesh wall.
Now, she's got a paddle to sell.

Rankled

There once was a player named Paul
Who always brought his own ball.
When no one said thank you,
Paul said, *I'm through!*
And left them with no ball at all.

Mischief Maker

What if a gnome roamed
on the court one day?
Would he feel at home
and decide to stay?
Would he grab a paddle
and insist that he play?
Or
Would he steal the ball
and just run away?

Liar

Robert said he didn't care if he won.
He always said he only played for fun.
But if that were true
then nobody knew
why losing made him come so undone.

Ball Hog

Peter played a mean game of pickleball
when the balls came over, he hit them all.
Since he couldn't share
no one would care
to play doubles with Peter that fall.

Dangerous Dennis

Dangerous Dennis dared dink in doubles.
Everyone feared his net game.
One day, Dennis darted too fast to the net.
They wheeled tangled Dennis away.

Ulterior Motive

Blanche brought cookies
to the court.
Baking was her last resort.

If she couldn't win fair and square,
she'd make them sluggish
with chocolate chunk cookies she'd prepared.

Fashion Sense

on-the-court fashion
is whatever helps your game
keep cool, collected

Posh Paul

Paul Peterson pickle-balled in a posh pantsuit.
One play day Paul peeped in his pantry.
The purple pantsuit had gone poof.
"Oh, pickles!"
Paul painfully perused his patterns:
pullovers, ponchos, pajamas.
Could Paul play in a parka? Perhaps.
Or, pair pedal pushers with a pullover.
But plain clothes never pacified Paul.
Paul's performance would lack panache.
Poor Paul had confused the court with a
catwalk. Pretentiousness had Paul in a pickle.
Finally, Paul paired a plum polo and pink
Pumas.
"Posh." He approved.

Two Bruces

One wore a green hat.
The other did not.
One played politely.
One had a killer shot.

One was still married.
The other was divorced.
One smiled easily.
The other's smile was forced.

One day the Bruces' game
was brutally tied
No matter how much
each Bruce had tried.

They argued and fussed
about every shot.
One said it was in,
The other said not.

That game there
it went on and on.
The sun was rising,
The sky nearing dawn.

One Bruce yawned.
The score was deuce.
The other sleepy-eyed guy
called for a truce.

Eventually they were both
willing to concede,
a thing that never happened:
They actually agreed.

You can go
round and round.
But if you want to move on,
Find common ground.

Going Places

True things to say you are doing
that are also playing pickleball:

getting some exercise
doing errands
meeting some friends
going to the park
putting some miles on your shoes
picking up a few things
managing stress
getting some steps
getting some running in
enjoying the fall weather
going shoe shopping
waiting in line
volunteering for kitchen duty

Smack

At pickleball, Sarah had once kicked ass,
But poor Sarah's game was at an impasse.
She'd talked too much smack.
Now, no one had her back.
Fate had caught up with Sarah at last.

the apologetic

First Sorry

First sorry of the season
happened when
I was standing too close
to the kitchen.
Next time, I vowed,
I would stay back
and help my partner
go on the attack.

Feelin' Guilty

I pull on my shoes,
dog wags tail. *Sorry*, I say,
pickleball today.

Seems to Be

According to Elton,
"sorry seems to be the hardest word"
but Midwest players know sorry slips out
after every point
some days
even after promises it won't
be uttered
again

sorry!

Hobbies Getting Jealous

With reading I get to live many lives
travel foreign lands and read for thrills.
But the time three-hundred pagers require
I would miss practicing pickleball skills.

I always wanted to strum the guitar.
Sadly, it's sitting at home in its case.
Fumbling fingers couldn't make me a star.
But with practice my serve became an ace

I've pedaled my road bike on the paved path.
But biking is often a solo sport.
Nothing compares to fun p-ballers have
when teaming up with their friends on the
court

I do wish I had more hours in the day.
Till then, I'll fiercely protect the time I can
play.

Other Words for Sorry

Sugar
Sh#!
Shoot
Shucks
Dang it
Darn it
Honey
Oh no
Oops
Oopsies
Ope
Boogers
Good Gravy
Snow

Swearing Jar

There should be
a swearing jar
of sorts
for every time
someone says
sorry
on the court.

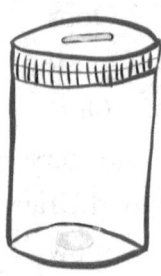

the coaches

Jim's Announcement

We wait like sheep
for our shepherd
to declare Sunday services
will begin
at 8:30.

Sunday Services Suffer

When rain pools on solemn courts,
We're being punished, Jim reports.
Tom asks when play will recommence.
Jim replies, *As soon as we repent.*

At First Sight

The first day I went to play,
I followed the directions
someone sent
on Facebook.

Go past the rec center
up the hill
just beyond
the tennis courts.

The empty acrylic fields
had weeds growing
from the cracks,
alley lines fading,
the vast flatlands
unkempt and forgotten.

Beyond that humble ghost town
were the pickleball courts.
They were bursting with players,
gallivanting among
all four courts

with people in line
watching on,
waiting anxiously to play,

For me and pickleball,
it was all
uphill
from there.

Unsolicited Advice

When the paddle rack paired June with May,
their willfulness got in the way.
June disliked May's tips.
May disliked June's quips.
They lost their game, needless to say.

the injured

Player Down

When a fifty-year old
decides to play like
they are twenty
something happens

a lunge
a dive
an I-WILL-NOT-LOSE attitude
ERUPTS

and then…

Ow!
Yowch!
That smarts!

What happened?

@!#!&—#

"9-1-1. What's your emergency?"

"We're at a pickleball court...."

The Moment

accidents happen in a moment
you can't control it
one wrong step
one fatal flaw
jaw dropped
wrecked
upset
you'll want that moment back
but you can't
take it back
you are trapped
with the aftermath
healing that can take months
chin up
it's only another broken moment
in a broken life
in a broken world
your life unfurled in a moment
now you must show what you are made of
chin up
you can meet this moment

Play Another Day

Keep your fiery spirit at bay.
Ignore naysayers who observe askance.
Live to play another day.

It's the hares -- not the tortoises -- who fall
prey,
When injured they must sit out the dance.
Keep your fiery spirit at bay.

Better players have limped away
Winning dislocations and tears by chance.
Live to play another day.

Though athletes always strive to play,
Injuries arrive by happenstance.
Keep your fiery spirit at bay.

A friendly game can go astray,
Injured players cannot advance.
Live to play another day.

Braggarts will have nothing to say
If they leave by ambulance,
Keep your fiery spirit at bay.

Why Isn't Tennis?

Why isn't tennis known for injuries?
Is it the more-sturdy mesh players meet
when rushing the net?

Is it the softer equipment --
no whiffle balls for tennis players --
they only use felt-covered orbs.

Is it the lengthier court
taking up more space and
keeping players farther apart,
out of harm's way?

Was tennis once
the new thing
everyone gravitated to?

Injuring players
in the honeymoon phase,
unsuspecting starstruck newbies
in love with their new craze
with no knowledge of
what could happen?

Did that also occur when tennis was
all the rage?
Will that be pickleball
someday?

Targeted Advertising

My wife and I stood
side by side
in the elevator,
riding up to her
PT appointment.
A poster above the floor buttons
showed two happy seniors
playing pickleball.

It was too close to the truth
and too close to my age.

*Must be a good time to be an
orthopedist*, my wife said,
stepping off the ride,
protecting her injured arm.

Agility Test

Maybe there should be a test
for newbies on the court,
something every player must pass,
to play this nimble sport.

First, back up ten steps
without falling on your seat,
daintily keep going
and stay up on your feet.

Walk through firing dodge balls
and still remain upright,
raising arms up as shields
deflecting balls in flight.

Go five rounds in a net
blocking plastic pucks
If they can't score a goal on you
then you are in luck!

Pickleball should be fun,
not see its players splat.
Test you're agile 'for the serve,
Don't be another stat.

And So It Goes

Where are you going?
--To get some exercise
You're going to play pickleball, aren't you?
--Um... yes.

Cares

care
careful
carefree
careless
caretaking
caregiving
uncaring
couldn't care less
could care less
care more
care

the spectators

The Sign

the red sign appeared
after Mel's dog chased a ball,
left it punctured, wet

Night

owls hoot overhead
sensing glorious silence
on the court below

In the Way

holey ball in breeze
is easy to catch, unless
it bonks off my nose

Retriever

Heat of game day calls
me to lie on the cool grass
under the maple

Toy

I chase tumbling leaves
each one a new crumbly toy,
bitten down, destroyed

Rat

Isn't a pickleball
just a whiffle ball
painted yellow or green?
Do manufacturers take us for fools?
Methinks I smell a rat.

Guilt

You're going to the court again?
--I need exercise.
Can't we just take a walk?
--It's not the same.
Fine... go ahead.

Spectator

squirrel, our greatest fan,
on haunches he watches us
volley back and forth

Transport

leaning patiently
against the cool chainlink fence
bike waits for game's end

the wannabes

Pickleball

So much depends upon[1]
a little plastic ball
with holes covering its surface
willing to be whacked around.

Homage to William Carlos Williams's *Red Wheelbarrow*, after first line "So much depends upon."

One Small Simile

the ball hurtles[2]
like a torpedo shot from a sub,
its target
a large painted square
amid a sea of swampy green,
only to be sent back over the net

Wild Paddler

Homage to Mary Oliver's *Wild Geese*, after first
line "You do not have to be good."

You do not have to be good.[3]
—I'm not.
You only need a paddle.
—You can use mine.
And to show up.
—I'll meet you there.
You could have been home watching
television.
—But don't.
You could have been reading a book.
—Or not.
But instead, you're serving. Lunging. Dancing.

On the court with a partner.

Meanwhile, people sit home eating ice cream
and watching *Law & Order* reruns.

Who's to say how we spend our time?

I live to be on the court,
a wild paddler,
never hoping for excellence,
just fun.

The Diehard

I think that I have never been[4]
so charmed by a game I rarely win

A game that draws all walks of life
and sadly injured my poor wife

A game where players leap and dance
when following their partner's stance

A game that you must win by two
even as daylight dims on you

Upon a court where shadows fall
and give excuse to miss the ball

This game is played by hacks like me,
But oh how I love my community.

Homage to Joyce Kilmer's *Trees* after first line:
"I think that I shall never see"

KRISTIN F. JOHNSON

The Paddle Not Chosen

Two paddles hung in a Dick's emporium,
and I--
I bought the most expensive one,
And that...
has made no difference.[5]

The Competitor

Because I tried hard to compete[6]
I hurt my poor elbow
the pain that followed not quite worth
a glorious winner's bellow.

Raised to ne'er give up a fight
I always gave my all
but for naught turns out this time
for one pickled game of ball.

Someday future I will say
arthritis now I suffer
because I could not let it go
and just be called a duffer.

Competitive spirits understand
the way things sometimes go
playing hard to not give in
you reap just what you sow.

the homages

please review

Thank you for reading my pickled pages. Speaking of pickles, I'm in one. I rely on word-of-mouth and reviews so people can learn about my books. Would you help me spread the word?

Please leave a rating or short review on Amazon, Goodreads, or Barnes & Noble. I read and appreciate every review!

Scan Me

Kristin's Amazon
Author Page

the author

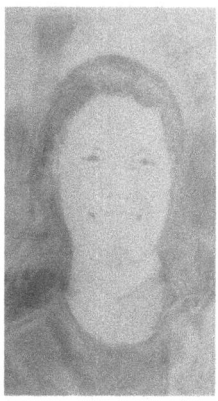

Author Self Portrait

Kristin F. Johnson prefers playing pickleball outdoors. She has published many poems in posh literary journals, including *The Talking Stick Journal*, *The Southwest Journal*, *Dust & Fire*, and *Haute Dish*. She also has ten books for kids, including the 5-star middle grade *Fearless*. Visit her at kfjbooks.com.

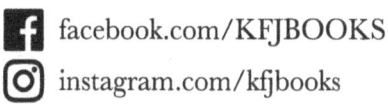

facebook.com/KFJBOOKS

instagram.com/kfjbooks

acknowledgements

Thank you to Jim Zusan and Tom Zusan. These two brothers taught me, and so many others, pickleball. They are our fearless, patient coaches. We appreciate you guys!

Special thanks to my friends at The Edge. It's been such a joy to be part of the community of pickleballers. And to the inaugural group of Writers Who Pickle: Aimée Bisonette, Joyce Sidman, and Jane O'Reilly. Remember: Safety first!

Thank you to my astute writing group for painstakingly reviewing drafts of every poem. You are incredibly helpful editors: Jacqueline West, Anne Greenwood Brown, Connie Kingrey Anderson, Jennifer Kaul, and Lauren Peck.

Thanks also to many other writer friends for reviewing drafts, especially Sarah Rose and Sandi Clough.

Thanks to my sister Laurie Jones for her endless encouragement and marketing advice!

Thanks to pickleballer (and actuary!) Steve Briggs for reviewing the manuscript from an experienced player's perspective.

Thank you to my friend Patty Scharf who asked me to play pickleball that first time. I didn't have a paddle to play, and she said I could use one of hers.

And, finally, thank you to Alisa for being so understanding every time I sneak off to the court.

also by kristin f. johnson

Fearless: A middle grade adventure